GOD, WE GOTTA TALK

REAL QUESTIONS, REAL FAITH, AND THE SEARCH FOR GOD IN A COMPLICATED WORLD

O. B. LEVY

AUTHOR'S NOTE

This book was not written from a place of certainty.

It was written from conversation.

From questions that surfaced in quiet moments, in hard seasons, and in conversations with people who wanted faith to feel real again. Questions that did not disappear with age, education, or experience. Questions that felt too honest for easy answers.

God, We Gotta Talk is not an attempt to explain everything or resolve every tension. It is an invitation to bring your real thoughts, doubts, frustrations, and hopes into conversation with God.

You do not have to clean up your questions before you ask them. You do not have to be certain to be sincere. Faith has always made room for honesty.

If you are reading this because you are searching, reconnecting, waiting, or simply tired, you are not alone. This book is meant to walk with you, not instruct you from a distance.

My hope is that these pages help you feel less isolated in your questions and more confident that God is not threatened by them.

The conversation does not end here.

It continues wherever you are willing to bring your whole self and keep talking.

HOW TO USE THIS BOOK

This book is not meant to be rushed.

It is not a checklist to complete or a test to pass. It is a conversation to enter and return to as often as you need.

You do not have to read this book in order. Some chapters may speak to you immediately. Others may not feel relevant yet. That is okay.

Read slowly. Pause when something stirs discomfort or recognition. Sit with questions that do not resolve quickly. Write in the margins if that helps you think honestly.

If you are reading alone, allow yourself to reflect without pressure. If you are reading with others, let the conversation be honest rather than impressive.

You are not expected to agree with everything here. You are invited to engage.

The goal is not certainty.

The goal is connection.

CONTENTS

1. GOD, WHY IS THE WORLD SO BROKEN?   1
    The Reality We Are Living In   2
    A Conversation God Has Heard Before   2
    How Things Broke in the First Place   3
    Creation Is Groaning and So Are We   4
    Where God Is in the Middle of It   4
    A Shift in Perspective   5
    Reflection Questions   5

2. GOD, WHY DO BAD PEOPLE SEEM TO WIN?   7
    What We Are Seeing   7
    A Question Scripture Does Not Avoid   8
    The Problem With What We Call Winning   9
    God Is Not Competing on Our Timeline   9
    What This Means for Us   10
    A Different Way to See It   11
    Reflection Questions   11

3. GOD, WHY DO YOU FEEL SILENT?   12
    What Silence Feels Like   12
    Voices That Asked the Same Question   13
    Silence Is Not Absence   13
    When God Delays on Purpose   14
    What Silence Produces in Us   15
    A Different Way to Listen   15
    Reflection Questions   16

4. GOD, WHY ARE WE SO ANXIOUS ALL THE TIME?   17
    The Weight We Carry   17
    What Jesus Noticed About Worry   18
    What Anxiety Reveals   19
    Peace That Does Not Make Sense   19
    When Anxiety and Faith Coexist   20

A Gentler Way Forward   20
Reflection Questions   21

5. GOD, WHY DO WE FEEL BEHIND IN LIFE?   22
The Pressure of Invisible Timelines   22
God's Timing Is Not Random   23
When Delay Feels Like Disappointment   24
Measuring Progress Differently   24
Trusting God With the Long View   25
Reflection Questions   25

6. GOD, WHY ARE WE BURNED OUT EVEN
WHEN WE'RE YOUNG?   26
The Culture That Keeps Us Running   26
What Jesus Said About Rest   27
Rest Is Not Laziness   27
When Burnout Reveals a Deeper Struggle   28
Learning a Slower Faith   29
Reflection Questions   29

7. GOD, WHY IS DATING SO CONFUSING NOW?   30
The Tension We Carry Into Relationships   30
How Culture Shapes the Confusion   31
Love That Requires More Than Feeling   32
When Waiting Feels Like Falling Behind   32
A Different Way to Approach Dating   33
Reflection Questions   33

8. GOD, WHY DON'T I KNOW MY PURPOSE YET?   35
The Anxiety of Undefined Identity   35
When Purpose Becomes Pressure   36
The Hidden Work of Waiting   37
Becoming Before Doing   37
A Gentler Understanding of Purpose   37
Reflection Questions   38

9. GOD, WHY DO I STILL STRUGGLE WITH THE
SAME THINGS?   39
The Shame That Grows in Repetition   39
When Scripture Feels Too Honest   40
The Difference Between Struggle and Surrender   40
God Is Not Surprised by Process   41

What Repeated Struggle Can Teach Us   42

A More Honest Kind of Hope   42

Reflection Questions   42

10. GOD, CAN YOU STILL USE ME AFTER WHAT I'VE DONE?   44

When Regret Becomes Identity   44

What Scripture Does Not Hide   45

The Lie of Disqualification   45

Grace That Goes Further Than We Expect   46

Being Used Does Not Mean Being Untouched   46

A Hope That Does Not Ignore the Past   46

Reflection Questions   47

11. GOD, IS IT OKAY TO DOUBT AND STILL BELIEVE?   48

The Fear Beneath the Question   48

Scripture Is More Honest Than We Expect   49

When Questions Are Invited   49

Doubt as a Form of Engagement   50

Faith That Breathes   50

A More Honest Definition of Belief   51

Reflection Questions   51

12. GOD, WHAT DOES WALKING WITH YOU ACTUALLY LOOK LIKE?   52

When Faith Feels Like a Concept   52

Walking, Not Performing   53

What Walking With God Includes   53

When Walking Feels Uneventful   54

A Faith That Can Stay   54

The Conversation Continues   55

Reflection Questions   55

EPILOGUE   56

God, We're Still Talking   56

Discussion Guide Appendix   59

About the Author   65

GOD, WHY IS THE WORLD SO BROKEN?

*G*od, we need to talk.

Because if we are being honest, the world feels heavy.

Not just heavy with bad news, but heavy in a way that settles into your chest and refuses to leave.

Every time we open our phones, there is another tragedy. Another injustice. Another reminder that something is not right. We see people hurting people. Systems failing people. Innocent lives cut short. Somewhere between scrolling and sighing, a question forms. Sometimes quietly. Sometimes sharp and demanding.

Why?

Why is the world like this?

Why does it feel like things are getting worse instead of better?

And if God is good, why does any of this exist at all?

These are not abstract questions. They are personal. They come from watching someone you love suffer. From losing a job. From seeing violence normalized. From realizing adulthood does not look like what you imagined. From waking up tired of being strong.

So God, why is the world so broken?

The Reality We Are Living In

We were promised progress. Technology. Convenience. Opportunity.

What many of us experience instead is anxiety, exhaustion, comparison, division, and a constant sense that something is off.

We are more connected than ever, yet loneliness is everywhere. We are informed in real time, yet overwhelmed and emotionally drained. We know what is happening across the globe, but we feel powerless to change much of anything.

When pain becomes constant, something shifts inside us. We either grow angry or we grow numb.

Some people blame humanity.

Some blame systems.

Some blame God.

Others quietly step away from faith altogether, not because they do not care, but because they care too deeply to accept easy answers.

If God is real, it feels like He owes us an explanation.

A Conversation God Has Heard Before

Here is something that matters. You are not the first person to ask this.

The Bible does not avoid pain or rush past suffering. Some of the most faithful people in Scripture questioned God directly, sometimes with frustration and sometimes through tears.

The prophet Habakkuk did not soften his words:

"O LORD, how long shall I cry for help, and you will
   not hear?
Or cry to you 'Violence!' and you will not save?"
   (Habakkuk 1:2, ESV)

That is not rebellion. That is honesty.

God did not reject Habakkuk for asking. He responded.

And before God speaks about fixing the world, He reveals something foundational. This brokenness was never the original design.

How Things Broke in the First Place

In the opening chapters of Genesis, the world is marked by harmony. There is peace between God and humanity, between people, and between humanity and creation.

Then choice enters the picture.

Genesis 3 describes the moment trust is broken. The consequences are not limited to one decision or one generation. They spread outward into every part of life.

"Cursed is the ground because of you...pain... toil..."
   (Genesis 3:17, ESV)

This is not God reacting in anger to curiosity. It is the natural outcome of separating from the source of life.

When our relationship with God fractures, everything else begins to fracture with it.

The pain we see today is not proof that God does not care. It is proof that brokenness does not stay contained.

Creation Is Groaning and So Are We

The apostle Paul describes what we experience but struggle to put into words:

> *"For the creation was subjected to futility...we know that the whole creation has been groaning together in the pains of childbirth until now." (Romans 8:20, 22, ESV)*

Groaning implies pain, but it also implies anticipation.
The world is not just broken.
It is waiting.
Waiting for restoration.
Waiting for redemption.
Waiting for God to complete what He promised to begin.
This means the chaos we experience is not random, and it is not permanent.

Where God Is in the Middle of It

This is usually the moment when people want a clean explanation. A formula. Something that makes suffering easier to understand.

Scripture offers something more honest.

God does not always explain why something happens in the moment. What He does consistently reveal is who He is in the middle of it.

He is not distant from suffering.

He steps into it.

The story of Scripture does not end with brokenness. It moves toward restoration.

"Behold, the dwelling place of God is with man...
He will wipe away every tear from their eyes,
and death shall be no more."
(Revelation 21:3–4, ESV)

God's response to a broken world is not abandonment. It is presence, redemption, and renewal.

A Shift in Perspective

Here is the difficult and hopeful truth.

God allows us to see how broken the world is so that we stop pretending it is home.

Pain awakens longing.

Brokenness points us toward restoration.

Unanswered questions invite deeper conversation.

This chapter does not solve the problem of suffering. But it opens the door to something essential.

God is not threatened by your questions.

He welcomes them.

If you have been angry, confused, disappointed, or exhausted, that does not disqualify you from faith.

It may be the beginning of an honest one.

Reflection Questions

1. When you look at the world today, what specifically feels broken to you?
2. Have you ever felt hesitant to bring hard questions or frustrations to God? Why?
3. Which part of this chapter resonated most with your current experience?

4. How does viewing brokenness as something temporary rather than final change the way you see suffering?
5. What is one question you want to bring into your ongoing conversation with God?

GOD, WHY DO BAD PEOPLE SEEM TO WIN?

*G*od, this one feels personal.

Because we are told that doing the right thing matters. That integrity counts. That kindness will come back around. Yet when we look at the world, it often feels like the opposite is true.

People who lie get promoted.

People who exploit others gain influence.

People who cause harm walk free.

And the people trying to live with honesty and compassion are left struggling, overlooked, or burned out.

So God, what are we supposed to do with that?

Why does it seem like the people who play fair lose, while the ones who cut corners thrive? Why does injustice feel so normal? And if You are just, why does justice take so long?

What We Are Seeing

We live in a world that rewards visibility, power, and results, not character.

We watch people build platforms on deception. We see

leaders avoid consequences. We watch systems protect those who already have power. And quietly, something begins to shift inside us.

We start to wonder if goodness is naive.

If integrity is optional.

If faith is practical at all.

Over time, resentment grows. Cynicism settles in. Some of us stop trying to do the right thing because it feels pointless.

And somewhere beneath that frustration is a deeper fear.

What if doing good actually puts us at a disadvantage?

A Question Scripture Does Not Avoid

This question is not new. It is ancient.

One of the most honest confessions in Scripture comes from someone who had followed God faithfully and still felt cheated.

The psalmist writes:

> *"But as for me, my feet had almost stumbled,*
> *my steps had nearly slipped.*
> *For I was envious of the arrogant*
> *when I saw the prosperity of the wicked." (Psalm 73:2–*
> *3, ESV)*

He is not pretending. He admits that watching unjust people succeed nearly pulled him away from God altogether.

He saw what we see.

Comfort without accountability.

Success without sacrifice.

Power without humility.

And for a moment, he wondered if faith was worth it.

The Problem With What We Call Winning

The turning point in Psalm 73 does not come when circumstances change. It comes when perspective does.

The psalmist writes:

> *"Until I went into the sanctuary of God;*
> *then I discerned their end." (Psalm 73:17, ESV)*

What looks like winning in the short term often hides a deeper loss.

Scripture repeatedly warns that unchecked success can harden hearts, distort values, and create an illusion of security.

Ecclesiastes explains part of the frustration we feel:

> *"Because the sentence against an evil deed is not*
> *executed speedily, the heart of the children of man is*
> *fully set to do evil." (Ecclesiastes 8:11, ESV)*

Delayed justice can feel like no justice at all. But Scripture reminds us that delay is not denial.

God Is Not Competing on Our Timeline

One of the hardest truths to accept is this. God does not operate on our sense of urgency.

We want immediate correction. Immediate consequences. Immediate balance.

God is patient, not because He ignores evil, but because He sees further than we do.

Paul writes:

> *"Beloved, never avenge yourselves, but leave it to the*

> *wrath of God, for it is written, 'Vengeance is mine, I*
> *will repay, says the Lord.'" (Romans 12:19, ESV)*

That verse is not permission to be passive. It is an invitation to trust that justice does not rest on our shoulders.

God does not overlook wrongdoing.

He does not forget harm.

He does not confuse success with righteousness.

But He also refuses to rush redemption.

What This Means for Us

If we are honest, part of our frustration comes from comparison.

We look sideways and measure our faithfulness against someone else's comfort. We assume that visible success equals blessing, and struggle equals failure.

Scripture challenges that assumption.

Jesus tells a story about a rich man who lived comfortably while ignoring the suffering around him. At the end of the story, Jesus makes it clear that earthly comfort did not reflect eternal favor.

> *"Child, remember that you in your lifetime received*
> *your good things..." (Luke 16:25, ESV)*

Winning, as the world defines it, is not the same as being right with God.

And losing, as it often feels to us, does not mean God has forgotten.

A Different Way to See It

Here is the quiet truth Scripture keeps pointing us toward:

God is not impressed by outcomes detached from character.

He is shaping who we are becoming, not just what we achieve.

Integrity may cost us speed, popularity, or comfort. But it anchors us in something that does not collapse when circumstances shift.

The question shifts from Why do bad people seem to win? to What kind of person am I becoming while I wait?

Faith does not guarantee fairness in the moment.

It promises that injustice does not get the final word.

Reflection Questions

1. Where have you seen injustice or dishonesty rewarded in ways that frustrated or discouraged you?
2. How has comparison affected the way you view your own faithfulness or progress?
3. What emotions come up for you when justice feels delayed?
4. How does Scripture's definition of winning differ from the world's definition?
5. What would it look like to trust God with justice instead of carrying that burden yourself?

GOD, WHY DO YOU FEEL SILENT?

God, this might be the hardest one to ask.

Because silence feels personal.

We can handle disappointment better than distance. We can wrestle with suffering more easily than absence. But when prayers seem to go unanswered, when heaven feels quiet, when words fall flat in the air, something inside us starts to ache.

We pray.

We wait.

We listen.

And nothing seems to happen.

So God, where are You?

Why do You feel silent when we need You most?

And how long are we supposed to keep believing when it feels like we are talking to ourselves?

What Silence Feels Like

Silence has a way of making us question everything.

We replay our prayers and wonder if we said something

wrong. We examine our lives, looking for hidden failures that might explain the distance. We scroll through verses about faith and confidence, wondering why our experience does not match what we read.

Eventually, doubt creeps in.

Maybe God is disappointed.

Maybe God is busy.

Maybe God is not listening at all.

And when silence lingers, it does not just affect our prayers. It shapes how we see ourselves and how we see God.

Voices That Asked the Same Question

Scripture does not pretend that silence is easy or rare.

David, a man described as being after God's own heart, cried out:

> "How long, O LORD? Will you forget me forever?
> How long will you hide your face from me?" (Psalm
>   13:1, ESV)

That question is not polite. It is desperate.

David did not whisper this in a moment of calm reflection. He spoke it from a place of waiting, confusion, and pain.

And God did not reject him for it.

Throughout Scripture, faithful people wrestle with silence. They wait. They question. They cry out. And they keep showing up, even when clarity does not come.

Silence Is Not Absence

One of the most damaging assumptions we make is equating silence with absence.

Just because God is quiet does not mean He is gone.

The book of Lamentations reminds us:

> *"For the Lord will not cast off forever,*
> *but, though he cause grief, he will have compassion*
> *according to the abundance of his steadfast love."*
> *(Lamentations 3:31–32, ESV)*

Silence does not cancel love.

Waiting does not negate care.

Sometimes God is quiet not because He is distant, but because He is doing something deeper than immediate answers.

When God Delays on Purpose

There is a moment in the Gospels that challenges our assumptions about silence.

When Jesus hears that His friend Lazarus is sick, He does not rush to help.

> *"Now Jesus loved Martha and her sister and Lazarus.*
> *So, when he heard that Lazarus was ill, he stayed two*
> *days longer..." (John 11:5–6, ESV)*

That sentence is unsettling.

Jesus loved them, so He waited.

His delay was not indifference. It was intentional. He was working toward a greater restoration than they could imagine, even though His silence caused real pain in the meantime.

This does not make waiting easy. But it reframes it.

Sometimes God is silent because He is preparing something we cannot yet see.

What Silence Produces in Us

Silence strips us of shortcuts.

When answers come quickly, faith can stay shallow. But when silence stretches on, something else begins to form.

Dependence.

Honesty.

Endurance.

Isaiah offers this reminder:

> *"Therefore the LORD waits to be gracious to you,*
> *and therefore he exalts himself to show mercy to you."*
> *(Isaiah 30:18, ESV)*

God's waiting and our waiting are often happening at the same time.

In the quiet, we are invited to sit with God rather than rush past Him. To trust His character when we do not understand His timing.

A Different Way to Listen

Silence invites a shift.

Instead of asking, Why is God not speaking,

we begin to ask, What is God shaping in me while I wait?

God often uses silence to loosen our grip on control and deepen our trust in His presence.

Silence is uncomfortable because it forces us to rely on who God is, not just what He gives.

And that kind of faith lasts.

Reflection Questions

1. When have you experienced silence from God that felt confusing or painful?
2. What assumptions do you tend to make when prayers seem unanswered?
3. How does seeing silence as intentional rather than absent change your perspective?
4. What might God be forming in you during a season of waiting?
5. What would it look like to remain present with God even without clear answers?

GOD, WHY ARE WE SO ANXIOUS ALL THE TIME?

*od, this one feels constant.

It is not tied to one moment or one crisis. It follows us through our days. It shows up when we wake up and when we try to fall asleep. It hums beneath conversations, deadlines, decisions, and expectations.

We feel anxious about our future.

About money.

About relationships.

About whether we are doing enough or becoming enough.

Even when things are going well, the tension does not fully leave. There is always something else to worry about, something else to manage, something else to prepare for.

So God, why are we so anxious all the time?

And why does it feel so hard to find peace?

The Weight We Carry

Anxiety thrives in a world that demands constant awareness.

We are expected to stay informed, productive, available, and improving. We are told to plan ahead while staying flexible. To

17

be ambitious but balanced. To be confident but humble. To rest, but not fall behind.

It is no wonder our minds feel crowded.

We carry concerns that previous generations never had to hold all at once. News travels instantly. Comparisons are endless. Mistakes are permanent online. And the pressure to keep up never really shuts off.

Anxiety becomes the background noise of life.

And eventually, it starts to feel normal.

What Jesus Noticed About Worry

Jesus was not unaware of anxiety. He spoke directly to it.

In the Sermon on the Mount, He addressed people who were worried about survival, provision, and the future. People who did not have safety nets or savings accounts.

He said:

> *"Therefore I tell you, do not be anxious about your life, what you will eat or what you will drink, nor about your body, what you will put on." (Matthew 6:25, ESV)*

This is not dismissal. It is an invitation.

Jesus continues by naming what anxiety does to us:

> *"And which of you by being anxious can add a single hour to his span of life?" (Matthew 6:27, ESV)*

Anxiety feels productive, but it does not actually protect us. It exhausts us while convincing us that worry is necessary.

What Anxiety Reveals

At its core, anxiety is not just about fear. It is about control.

We become anxious when we feel responsible for outcomes we cannot guarantee. When we believe everything depends on us. When rest feels risky and trust feels irresponsible.

Peter writes:

> *"Casting all your anxieties on him, because he cares for you." (1 Peter 5:7, ESV)*

That verse assumes something important. Anxiety is something we are carrying.

God does not shame us for holding it. He invites us to release it.

But release is hard when anxiety has become familiar.

Peace That Does Not Make Sense

Paul writes to the church in Philippi from prison, not from comfort or stability.

And still, he says:

> *"Do not be anxious about anything, but in everything by prayer and supplication with thanksgiving let your requests be made known to God." (Philippians 4:6, ESV)*

He does not say anxiety will disappear instantly. He describes what follows:

> *"And the peace of God, which surpasses all understanding, will guard your hearts and your minds in Christ Jesus." (Philippians 4:7, ESV)*

Peace does not always remove the situation.

Sometimes it guards us in the middle of it.

This kind of peace does not come from certainty. It comes from surrender.

When Anxiety and Faith Coexist

Many of us assume that feeling anxious means we are failing spiritually.

Scripture tells a different story.

The psalmist admits:

> *"When the cares of my heart are many,*
> *your consolations cheer my soul." (Psalm 94:19, ESV)*

God does not wait for anxiety to disappear before offering comfort. He meets us while it is still present.

Faith does not mean the absence of anxious thoughts.

It means choosing where to bring them.

A Gentler Way Forward

Anxiety does not make you weak. It makes you human.

But carrying it alone will eventually wear you down.

God does not promise a life without uncertainty. He promises His presence in the middle of it.

The invitation is not to ignore anxiety, but to notice what it is pointing toward.

Where are you trying to hold everything together on your own?

What are you afraid will fall apart if you stop worrying?

Peace begins when we loosen our grip and let God carry what we were never meant to hold alone.

Reflection Questions

1. What are the most common sources of anxiety in your life right now?
2. How has constant pressure shaped the way you think about rest and trust?
3. In what ways does anxiety show up as a need for control?
4. What would it look like to bring anxious thoughts to God rather than managing them alone?
5. Where might God be inviting you into peace that does not depend on certainty?

GOD, WHY DO WE FEEL BEHIND IN LIFE?

❧

*G*od, this one sneaks up on us.

It does not always announce itself as failure. Sometimes it shows up quietly, in conversations and comparisons, in moments when we realize we are not where we thought we would be by now.

We thought we would be more settled.

More confident.

More accomplished.

Instead, many of us feel like we are constantly catching up. Watching others move forward while we stay in place. Wondering if we missed a turn somewhere along the way.

So God, why do we feel behind in life?

And how do we stop measuring ourselves against a timeline that never seems to work in our favor?

The Pressure of Invisible Timelines

No one ever hands us a schedule for how life is supposed to unfold. Yet somehow, we all seem to know when we think we should have certain things figured out.

By this age, we should know our purpose.

By now, we should be financially stable.

At this point, we should have meaningful relationships locked in.

These expectations do not usually come from God. They come from culture, comparison, and quiet assumptions we absorb over time.

Social media does not help. We see highlights, milestones, announcements, and celebrations. Rarely do we see the uncertainty, doubt, or waiting behind them.

And when our lives do not match what we think is normal, we start to believe something is wrong with us.

God's Timing Is Not Random

Scripture repeatedly pushes back against the idea that life should unfold on our schedule.

Paul writes:

> *"But when the fullness of time had come, God sent forth his Son..." (Galatians 4:4, ESV)*

That phrase matters. Fullness of time.

God did not act early.

He did not act late.

He acted with intention.

Waiting is not wasted time in God's economy. It is often preparation.

The psalmist reminds us:

> *"Be still before the LORD and wait patiently for him."*
> *(Psalm 37:7, ESV)*

Waiting is rarely comfortable, but it is rarely empty.

When Delay Feels Like Disappointment

Feeling behind often comes with grief.

We grieve plans that did not work out. Versions of ourselves we thought we would become. Opportunities that never opened.

Mary and Martha felt this when Jesus arrived after their brother had died.

Martha said:

> *"Lord, if you had been here, my brother would not have died." (John 11:21, ESV)*

Her words are heavy with disappointment. She believed Jesus had power. She just did not understand His timing.

Jesus did not correct her grief.

He met her in it.

Delay does not mean God is indifferent. Sometimes it means He is working in ways we cannot yet see.

Measuring Progress Differently

One of the reasons we feel behind is because we measure progress by visibility.

We value results over growth. Outcomes over obedience. Speed over faithfulness.

Scripture invites us to measure differently.

> *"The heart of man plans his way,*
> *but the LORD establishes his steps." (Proverbs*
> *16:9, ESV)*

We may feel stalled, but God may be redirecting. We may

feel late, but God may be aligning things we cannot yet understand.

Progress in God's kingdom is often quieter than we expect.

Trusting God With the Long View

Feeling behind can tempt us to rush decisions. To settle for things that look like movement but do not bring peace. To compare ourselves into discouragement.

God invites us to trust His long view.

Waiting is not passive.

It is active trust.

It requires believing that God is not forgetting us, overlooking us, or falling behind Himself.

He is attentive.

He is deliberate.

He is present.

And His timing is shaped by wisdom, not pressure.

Reflection Questions

1. In what areas of your life do you most often feel behind?
2. What timelines or expectations have influenced how you evaluate your progress?
3. How does comparing your life to others affect your sense of worth or peace?
4. What might God be developing in you during seasons that feel slow or uncertain?
5. What would it look like to trust God with your timing instead of rushing ahead?

GOD, WHY ARE WE BURNED OUT EVEN WHEN WE'RE YOUNG?

*G*od, this feels confusing.

We are not supposed to be this tired yet. We are still early in our lives, still figuring things out, still building. And yet, many of us feel drained before we ever feel established.

We wake up exhausted.

We push through our days on autopilot.

We fall into bed already dreading tomorrow.

It is not just physical tiredness. It is emotional and mental exhaustion. A sense that no matter how much we do, it is never enough.

So God, why are we burned out even when we are young?

And how did life become this heavy so quickly?

The Culture That Keeps Us Running

Burnout thrives in a culture that celebrates constant motion.

We are encouraged to hustle, optimize, and maximize every moment. Rest is treated like a reward instead of a necessity. Slowing down feels irresponsible. Saying no feels like failure.

We carry expectations to be productive, successful, and available all at once. To pursue our goals while staying connected, informed, and emotionally present.

Over time, the pace becomes unsustainable.

Burnout is not always the result of doing too much at once. Often, it comes from doing too much for too long without rest.

What Jesus Said About Rest

Jesus understood exhaustion.

He watched crowds press in. He listened to constant need. He carried responsibility, grief, and purpose.

And still, He said:

> *"Come to me, all who labor and are heavy laden, and I*
> *will give you rest." (Matthew 11:28, ESV)*

This invitation is not conditional. It is not reserved for people who have earned rest.

Jesus continues:

> *"Take my yoke upon you, and learn from me...*
> *For my yoke is easy, and my burden is light." (Matthew*
> *11:29–30, ESV)*

Burnout often happens when we carry burdens we were never meant to shoulder alone.

Rest Is Not Laziness

One of the lies we absorb is that rest equals weakness.

Scripture tells a different story.

God established rest as part of creation itself. In the Ten

Commandments, He instructed His people to observe a day of rest:

> *"Remember the Sabbath day, to keep it holy." (Exodus 20:8, ESV)*

Rest was not an afterthought. It was a rhythm.

When Jesus sent His disciples out to serve, He also called them back to rest:

> *"Come away by yourselves to a desolate place and rest a while." (Mark 6:31, ESV)*

Rest is not quitting.
It is obedience.

When Burnout Reveals a Deeper Struggle

Burnout often exposes something beneath the exhaustion.

We may be trying to prove our worth through productivity. We may fear falling behind or being forgotten. We may believe that if we stop, everything will fall apart.

The psalmist writes:

> *"It is in vain that you rise up early and go late to rest,*
> *eating the bread of anxious toil;*
> *for he gives to his beloved sleep." (Psalm 127:2, ESV)*

That verse challenges our assumptions. God does not measure our value by output.

Burnout can be a signal, not a failure. An invitation to examine what is driving us.

Learning a Slower Faith

Following God does not require constant exhaustion.

Jesus did not rush. He withdrew to pray. He rested. He trusted the Father's timing.

A slower faith does not mean a less committed one. It means a more sustainable one.

God invites us to lay down unrealistic expectations and receive rest as a gift, not something to be earned.

Reflection Questions

1. Where do you notice burnout showing up most clearly in your life?
2. What messages about productivity and rest have shaped how you view your worth?
3. What makes rest feel difficult or uncomfortable for you?
4. How does Jesus' invitation to rest challenge your current pace of life?
5. What is one small way you could begin to honor rest as obedience rather than indulgence?

GOD, WHY IS DATING
SO CONFUSING NOW?

*od, this one leaves us tired before it leaves us hopeful.

Because dating no longer feels simple. It feels layered. Complicated. Heavy in ways we did not expect.

We want connection, but we are afraid of vulnerability.

We want commitment, but we fear choosing wrong.

We want intimacy, but we hesitate to be fully known.

So we protect ourselves. We keep things casual. We avoid defining anything too clearly. We say we are fine with uncertainty, even when it quietly wears us down.

And after a while, dating stops feeling like discovery and starts feeling like survival.

So God, why is dating so confusing now?

Why does something meant to bring companionship so often leave us anxious, guarded, and unsure of ourselves?

The Tension We Carry Into Relationships

Dating today often begins with hope and quickly turns into calculation.

We wonder how much to share. How soon is too soon. Whether caring more makes us vulnerable or foolish. We try to read between texts, interpret silence, and manage expectations that were never spoken aloud.

We are told to protect our hearts, but not too much.

To be honest, but not intense.

To be independent, but not distant.

The result is emotional exhaustion.

We want love, but we do not want to be hurt again. We want clarity, but we fear the risk that clarity requires. So we stay halfway in. Close enough to feel something, far enough to escape if it falls apart.

And slowly, confusion replaces trust.

How Culture Shapes the Confusion

Much of our dating confusion does not come from desire. It comes from messages we absorb without realizing it.

We live in a culture that treats people as options and relationships as upgrades. One swipe away from someone new. One disagreement away from moving on.

Commitment is often framed as loss rather than depth. Vulnerability is seen as weakness. And patience feels unnecessary when everything else in life moves quickly.

Scripture offers a different posture:

> *"Keep your heart with all vigilance, for from it flow the springs of life." (Proverbs 4:23, ESV)*

Guarding your heart does not mean closing it off. It means recognizing that what you give access to shapes you.

When dating lacks intention, confusion grows.

Love That Requires More Than Feeling

Scripture does not deny attraction or desire. But it refuses to define love by emotion alone.

Paul writes words we often hear at weddings but rarely apply to dating:

> *"Love is patient and kind...*
> *it does not insist on its own way."* (1 Corinthians 13:4–
> 5, ESV)

That kind of love takes time. It requires honesty. It asks for maturity.

It also demands clarity.

From the beginning, God framed relationship as something meaningful, not casual:

> *"It is not good that the man should be alone."* (Genesis
> 2:18, ESV)

Companionship was meant to bring support and wholeness, not constant anxiety or self doubt.

When dating leaves us shrinking, second guessing, or pretending, something is misaligned.

When Waiting Feels Like Falling Behind

One of the hardest parts of dating is waiting.

Waiting for clarity.

Waiting for the right person.

Waiting for timing to make sense.

Waiting can feel like being left behind while others move forward.

Scripture speaks gently but firmly about timing:

"Do not stir up or awaken love until it so desires." (Song of Solomon 8:4, ESV)

This is not restriction. It is protection.

Rushed love often leads to regret. Love built slowly has space to grow roots.

Waiting does not mean God is withholding something good. It may mean He is preserving you for something healthier.

A Different Way to Approach Dating

What if dating was less about performing and more about discernment?

Less about proving your worth and more about paying attention to peace.

Dating was never meant to cost you your sense of self. It was never meant to leave you chronically anxious or unsure of your value.

God does not ask you to abandon wisdom for romance.

He does not require confusion as the price of connection.

Clarity may not come quickly, but peace often accompanies truth.

Reflection Questions

1. What parts of dating feel most draining or confusing for you right now?
2. How have cultural expectations shaped the way you approach relationships?
3. Where do you notice yourself holding back out of fear rather than wisdom?
4. How does Scripture's definition of love challenge your current assumptions?

O. B. LEVY

5. What would it look like to pursue dating with
   intention rather than pressure?

GOD, WHY DON'T I
KNOW MY PURPOSE YET?

*od, this question feels unsettling.

Not because we expect to have everything figured out, but because we feel like we should have *something* figured out by now.

We watch people talk confidently about their calling. We see peers settle into careers, passions, and paths that look intentional. And quietly, we wonder why clarity seems to come so easily to everyone else.

We feel pressure to explain ourselves. To justify where we are. To prove that our uncertainty is temporary.

So God, why don't I know my purpose yet?

Why does it feel like I am wandering while everyone else is moving forward?

The Anxiety of Undefined Identity

Purpose has become more than direction. It has become identity.

We are asked what we do, what we plan to do, and where we

see ourselves going. And over time, those questions begin to feel like measures of worth.

When answers are unclear, insecurity grows.

We start to believe that uncertainty means we are failing. That delay means we are behind. That not knowing means something is missing in us.

But Scripture offers a different starting point.

Before God ever speaks about calling, He speaks about knowing.

> *"Before I formed you in the womb I knew you." (Jeremiah 1:5, ESV)*

Being known comes before being sent.

When Purpose Becomes Pressure

Much of our frustration comes from how purpose is framed.

We are taught to find it, chase it, and achieve it. To make our lives meaningful as quickly as possible. Waiting feels irresponsible. Uncertainty feels dangerous.

But Scripture rarely presents purpose as something discovered all at once.

Instead, it presents a pattern of obedience, trust, and gradual unfolding.

Micah captures it simply:

> *"He has told you, O man, what is good...*
> *to do justice, and to love kindness, and to walk humbly*
> *with your God." (Micah 6:8, ESV)*

Purpose begins with posture, not position.

The Hidden Work of Waiting

Waiting is uncomfortable because it feels unproductive.

We want movement. We want progress we can measure. We want reassurance that time is not being wasted.

But Scripture consistently shows God doing deep work in unseen seasons.

David spent years waiting to become king. Moses spent decades in obscurity. The disciples followed Jesus without knowing where the path would lead.

Waiting was not a pause in their story. It was preparation.

Purpose is often shaped quietly before it is expressed publicly.

Becoming Before Doing

One of the most freeing truths Scripture offers is this.

God cares deeply about who you are becoming.

Jesus did not rush His ministry. He lived, worked, and waited before stepping fully into His calling.

Purpose is not a title you arrive at.

It is a life you grow into.

The psalmist writes:

> *"Wait for the LORD; be strong, and let your heart take*
> *courage;*
> *wait for the LORD." (Psalm 27:14, ESV)*

Waiting is not wasted when God is involved.

A Gentler Understanding of Purpose

What if purpose is less about finding the right path and more about walking faithfully where you are?

What if clarity comes through obedience rather than planning?

God does not require certainty before relationship. He invites trust.

You are not late.

You are not overlooked.

You are not failing because you do not yet have all the answers.

God is not in a hurry.

Reflection Questions

1. In what ways do you feel pressure to define your purpose right now?
2. How have comparison and expectation shaped your sense of identity?
3. What fears surface when you think about waiting?
4. How does Scripture's view of purpose differ from the one you have absorbed?
5. What does faithfulness look like for you in this current season?

GOD, WHY DO I STILL STRUGGLE WITH THE SAME THINGS?

*G*od, this one feels defeating.

Because at some point, we expected progress to look different. We thought growth would mean leaving certain struggles behind. That maturity would feel cleaner. That faith would make some battles disappear altogether.

But here we are, still wrestling with familiar habits. Still tripping over the same weaknesses. Still asking forgiveness for things we thought we had already moved past.

And the longer it goes on, the quieter the question becomes, but the heavier it feels.

God, why do I still struggle with the same things?

And what does it say about me that I have not changed more by now?

The Shame That Grows in Repetition

There is a unique kind of discouragement that comes from repeated struggle.

The first time, we feel conviction.

The second time, frustration.

After that, shame.

We stop talking about it. We assume everyone else is doing better than we are. We begin to wonder if something is fundamentally wrong with us.

We tell ourselves we should know better by now.

We should be stronger.

We should have moved on.

And slowly, struggle stops feeling like part of growth and starts feeling like proof of failure.

When Scripture Feels Too Honest

One of the most surprising moments in Scripture comes from the apostle Paul.

Paul was faithful, disciplined, and deeply committed to God. And yet, he writes words that feel uncomfortably familiar:

> *"For I do not understand my own actions. For I do not do what I want, but I do the very thing I hate."*
> *(Romans 7:15, ESV)*

Paul does not minimize the struggle. He does not pretend it should not be happening. He names it plainly.

This is not a new believer speaking.

This is not someone lacking effort.

This is someone growing honestly.

Struggle, it turns out, is not evidence of insincerity.

The Difference Between Struggle and Surrender

There is an important distinction Scripture makes that we often blur.

Struggling is not the same as surrendering.

The fact that something bothers you, that you want change, that you keep returning to God rather than walking away, matters deeply.

Proverbs reminds us:

> *"For the righteous falls seven times and rises again."*
> *(Proverbs 24:16, ESV)*

Righteousness is not defined by never falling.

It is defined by getting back up.

Growth is rarely a straight line. It is often marked by resistance, repetition, and return.

God Is Not Surprised by Process

One of the lies shame tells us is that God expected more from us by now.

Scripture tells a different story.

John writes:

> *"If we confess our sins, he is faithful and just to forgive us our sins and to cleanse us from all unrighteousness." (1 John 1:9, ESV)*

That verse does not come with a limit.

It does not suggest God grows tired of forgiving.

It assumes ongoing need.

And Paul offers this promise:

> *"He who began a good work in you will bring it to completion." (Philippians 1:6, ESV)*

Completion implies process.

God is committed to finishing what He started, even when growth feels slow and uneven.

What Repeated Struggle Can Teach Us

Sometimes the struggle itself reveals what we rely on.

It shows us where we reach for comfort instead of trust. Where we try to manage pain on our own. Where healing still needs time.

God does not use struggle to shame us.

He uses it to invite us deeper.

Grace does not excuse sin, but it does remove the fear that keeps us stuck in it.

A More Honest Kind of Hope

Hope does not come from pretending struggle is gone.

It comes from knowing you are not abandoned in it.

Faith is not proven by perfection.

It is revealed in persistence.

Every time you turn back to God, even with the same confession, you are choosing relationship over isolation.

And that choice matters.

Reflection Questions

1. What recurring struggle feels most discouraging for you right now?
2. How has shame affected the way you talk to God about it?
3. What difference do you see between struggling and giving up?

4. How does Scripture's honesty about process change your expectations of growth?
5. What would it look like to bring your struggle into the light instead of hiding it?

GOD, CAN YOU STILL USE
ME AFTER WHAT I'VE DONE?

❦

*G*od, this question carries weight.

Because some mistakes do not fade quietly into the past. They linger. They resurface when we least expect them. They shape how we see ourselves, even after we have moved forward in other areas of life.

We replay moments we wish we could undo. Words we cannot take back. Choices we would change if we could. And over time, regret stops being something we feel and starts becoming something we believe about ourselves.

So God, can You still use me after what I've done?

Or did I disqualify myself somewhere along the way?

When Regret Becomes Identity

Regret has a way of rewriting our story.

At first, it shows up as remorse. Then as shame. Eventually, it becomes a quiet conclusion we live with. We stop expecting much from ourselves. We assume God expects even less.

We tell ourselves that grace may cover us, but purpose probably passed us by. That forgiveness might be possible, but usefulness is not.

We believe there is a version of us God wanted to use, and we are not that version anymore.

And that belief is heavy.

What Scripture Does Not Hide

The Bible does not avoid failure. It records it in detail.

David was chosen by God and later committed grave sin. His regret was deep and public. He did not minimize it. He prayed honestly:

> *"Create in me a clean heart, O God,*
> *and renew a right spirit within me." (Psalm 51:10, ESV)*

David did not ask to be erased.
He asked to be restored.
And God did not discard him.

The Lie of Disqualification

One of the most damaging assumptions we make is that usefulness depends on a clean past.

Scripture challenges that idea repeatedly.

Jesus tells a story about a son who leaves home, wastes everything, and returns with nothing but regret. He expects rejection. He prepares to be treated like a servant.

Instead, Scripture says:

> *"While he was still a long way off, his father saw him*
> *and felt compassion, and ran and embraced him."*
> *(Luke 15:20, ESV)*

The father does not hesitate.
He does not lecture.
He restores relationship immediately.
That story is not about ignoring consequences.
It is about refusing to let failure define the future.

Grace That Goes Further Than We Expect

Paul writes words that feel almost too generous:

> *"There is therefore now no condemnation for those who are in Christ Jesus." (Romans 8:1, ESV)*

No condemnation does not mean no responsibility.
It means no sentence.
God does not erase our stories. He redeems them.
And redemption often reaches places shame tells us are beyond repair.

Being Used Does Not Mean Being Untouched

Sometimes we imagine being used by God means being polished, unmarked, and impressive.

Scripture offers a different picture.

God consistently works through people who are aware of their weakness. Who remember where they came from. Who know what grace feels like because they have needed it deeply.

Your past does not disqualify you.

It may be the very place God meets others through you.

A Hope That Does Not Ignore the Past

Healing does not require pretending the past did not happen.

It requires trusting that God can bring meaning even out of what we regret.

God does not rush restoration.

He walks it with us.

And usefulness in God's kingdom is not about having a flawless story.

It is about offering a redeemed one.

Reflection Questions

1. What regrets feel hardest to release right now?
2. How have past mistakes shaped the way you see yourself?
3. Where do you feel tempted to believe you are disqualified?
4. How does Scripture challenge your understanding of redemption?
5. What would it look like to trust God with your story as it is, not as you wish it were?

GOD, IS IT OKAY TO DOUBT AND STILL BELIEVE?

God, this question feels risky.

Because doubt is often treated like a failure. Something to hide. Something to fix quickly before it turns into something worse.

We learn how to say the right things. How to sound confident even when we are not. How to smile through questions we do not know how to answer.

And over time, we start to wonder if belief requires certainty.

If faith means never questioning.

If doubt is a sign that something is wrong with us.

So God, is it okay to doubt and still believe?

Or does doubt quietly push us outside the boundaries of faith?

The Fear Beneath the Question

Most of us are not afraid of doubt itself. We are afraid of where it might lead.

We worry that questions will unravel belief. That honesty

will cost us community. That naming uncertainty will expose us as weaker or less spiritual than everyone else.

So we keep doubts private. We wrestle alone. We tell ourselves we should already know the answers by now.

And that isolation makes doubt heavier than it needs to be.

Scripture Is More Honest Than We Expect

The Bible does not present faith as unshakable confidence.

It presents faith as trust formed in the middle of uncertainty.

A father once brought his hurting child to Jesus and spoke words that still feel painfully relevant:

> *"I believe; help my unbelief!" (Mark 9:24, ESV)*

Jesus did not rebuke him.

He did not demand stronger faith.

He responded with compassion.

That moment matters.

It tells us that belief and doubt are not always opposites. Sometimes they exist side by side in the same breath.

When Questions Are Invited

One of the most misunderstood figures in Scripture is Thomas.

After Jesus' resurrection, Thomas could not believe without seeing for himself. He questioned what others accepted.

Jesus did not shame him.

> *"Put your finger here, and see my hands...*
> *Do not disbelieve, but believe." (John 20:27, ESV)*

Jesus met Thomas where he was.

He did not demand blind faith.

He offered presence.

That tells us something important about God's posture toward doubt.

God is not threatened by honest questions.

Doubt as a Form of Engagement

There is a difference between doubt that pushes God away and doubt that leans in.

Scripture acknowledges this distinction:

> *"Have mercy on those who doubt." (Jude 1:22, ESV)*

That verse assumes doubt will exist within the community of faith.

Doubt becomes destructive when it isolates us.

It becomes transformative when it drives us toward truth.

Questions can deepen faith when they are brought into relationship instead of buried in shame.

Faith That Breathes

Faith was never meant to be brittle.

A faith that cannot withstand questions will eventually collapse under pressure. A faith that can breathe, wrestle, and grow becomes resilient.

Belief is not certainty about everything.

It is trust in Someone, even when everything does not make sense.

God does not ask us to silence our questions.

He asks us to bring them to Him.

A More Honest Definition of Belief

Belief is not pretending.

It is choosing to stay.

Staying when answers are incomplete.

Staying when certainty fades.

Staying in relationship even when understanding lags behind.

Doubt does not disqualify faith.

Avoiding God does.

And even then, Scripture tells us God pursues.

Reflection Questions

1. What doubts have you felt afraid to name or admit?
2. How were you taught to view doubt growing up?
3. What difference do you see between doubt that isolates and doubt that seeks?
4. How does Jesus' response to questioning shape your view of faith?
5. What would it look like to bring your questions into conversation with God rather than hiding them?

GOD, WHAT DOES WALKING WITH YOU ACTUALLY LOOK LIKE?

*G*od, after all these questions, this one feels necessary.

Because we have talked about pain, doubt, waiting, regret, anxiety, and confusion. We have named the weight we carry and the questions we bring into this conversation. And somewhere along the way, another question begins to form.

What now?

What does faith look like when life is still unresolved?

When answers are incomplete?

When the world remains broken and we remain human?

God, what does walking with You actually look like?

When Faith Feels Like a Concept

For many of us, faith has been defined by moments.

A prayer we prayed once.

A decision we made years ago.

A belief we say we hold.

But walking implies movement. Ongoing presence. Daily choice.

We know how to attend church. We know how to read verses. We know how to agree with ideas about God.

But relationship is different.

Relationship requires attention, honesty, and time.

And that is where many of us feel unsure.

Walking, Not Performing

Scripture consistently pulls faith out of the realm of performance.

God does not ask us to impress Him. He asks us to stay close.

The prophet Micah says it simply:

"To walk humbly with your God." (Micah 6:8, ESV)

Walking humbly assumes imperfection.

It assumes dependence.

It assumes ongoing need.

Jesus echoes this relational posture when He says:

"Abide in me, and I in you." (John 15:4, ESV)

Abiding is not striving.

It is remaining.

Faith grows through proximity, not pressure.

What Walking With God Includes

Walking with God includes ordinary moments.

It looks like prayer that is honest rather than polished. Scripture read slowly rather than rushed. Silence that feels awkward but stays open.

It includes bringing anxiety instead of hiding it. Bringing

doubt instead of burying it. Bringing failure instead of pretending it did not happen.

The psalmist writes:

> *"You make known to me the path of life;*
> *in your presence there is fullness of joy." (Psalm*
> *   16:11, ESV)*

Joy is found in presence, not perfection.

When Walking Feels Uneventful

One of the quiet disappointments of faith is that walking with God does not always feel dramatic.

There are seasons where nothing feels new. Where growth is subtle. Where faith feels steady but unspectacular.

That does not mean God is absent.

Paul reminds us:

> *"As you received Christ Jesus the Lord, so walk in him."*
> *(Colossians 2:6, ESV)*

Walking implies continuity.
Not restarting every time we fail.
Not proving ourselves again.
Continuing.
Faith is sustained through consistency more than intensity.

A Faith That Can Stay

Walking with God means choosing to stay in relationship, even when understanding lags behind experience.

It means trusting God's character when clarity is missing. Returning when we wander. Showing up when we feel unsure.

God is not asking for flawless devotion.

He is asking for presence.

And presence is something we can offer, even on hard days.

The Conversation Continues

This book does not end with everything resolved.

Because faith does not work that way.

The questions may change, but the conversation continues. And that is not a weakness. It is the shape of relationship.

God is not intimidated by ongoing dialogue.

He welcomes it.

Walking with God looks like continuing to talk, listen, wait, trust, and return.

Again and again.

Reflection Questions

1. How have you typically defined what it means to walk with God?
2. Where has faith felt more like performance than relationship?
3. What practices help you stay present with God, even when clarity is missing?
4. How does viewing faith as walking rather than arriving change your expectations?
5. What would it look like to keep this conversation with God going beyond these pages?

God, we have questions.

We bring them honestly.

And we keep walking.

EPILOGUE

God, We're Still Talking

God,
If we are honest, we do not close this book with answers neatly lined up.

Some questions remain. Some wounds are still tender. Some paths are still unclear.

But we close it still talking to You.

We brought our frustration.

Our doubt.

Our waiting.

Our fear that we were falling behind or falling short.

We brought the parts of ourselves we usually hide.

The parts we thought faith required us to clean up first.

And You did not turn away.

You listened.

You stayed.

You met us in the tension instead of rushing us through it.

So here we are, God.

Not fixed.

Not finished.

But present.

Teach us how to keep coming back when life feels heavy.

How to trust You when clarity does not come quickly.

How to rest when the world tells us to run faster.

How to believe when faith feels quiet instead of confident.

Help us remember that walking with You is not about having the right words, but about staying in the conversation.

When we feel anxious, remind us You are near.

When we feel behind, remind us You are not in a hurry.

When we doubt, remind us You are not offended.

When we fail, remind us You are still working.

We do not ask for easy lives.

We ask for honest faith.

Faith that can ask questions without fear.

Faith that can wait without giving up.

Faith that keeps showing up, even when the way forward feels slow.

God, thank You for meeting us here.

Thank You for listening.

Thank You for staying.

We will keep talking.

We will keep walking.

And we trust that You will keep meeting us along the way.

Amen.

DISCUSSION GUIDE APPENDIX

This guide is designed for individual reflection or group conversation. Use what serves you. Leave what does not.

There are no correct answers here. The goal is honesty.

General Guidelines

- Let people speak without interruption

- Resist fixing or correcting one another

- Allow silence when needed

- Keep the conversation grounded in lived experience

Chapter 1 — God, Why Is the World So Broken?

1. What feels most broken in the world right now to you personally?

2. How have you responded to suffering in your own life?

3. What questions about God surface when pain feels constant?

Chapter 2 — God, Why Do Bad People Seem to Win?

1. Where have you seen injustice rewarded?

2. How has comparison affected your faith?

3. What does trusting God with justice look like in real life?

Chapter 3 — God, Why Do You Feel Silent?

1. When have you experienced silence from God?

2. What assumptions do you make during waiting seasons?

3. How do you usually respond to unanswered prayers?

Chapter 4 — God, Why Are We So Anxious All the Time?

1. What anxiety shows up most often for you?

2. How does control play a role in your worry?

3. What helps you experience peace, even briefly?

Chapter 5 — God, Why Do We Feel Behind in Life?

1. Where do you feel behind right now?

2. What timelines influence your self worth?

3. How might waiting be forming you?

Chapter 6 — God, Why Are We Burned Out Even When We're Young?

1. What contributes most to your exhaustion?

2. How do you view rest?

3. What would it look like to treat rest as obedience?

Chapter 7 — God, Why Is Dating So Confusing Now?

1. What has made dating feel difficult or draining?

2. How do fear and self protection show up in relationships?

3. What does intentionality look like for you?

Chapter 8 — God, Why Don't I Know My Purpose Yet?

1. What pressure do you feel to have clarity?

2. How do you define purpose?

3. What does faithfulness look like in this season?

Chapter 9 — God, Why Do I Still Struggle With the Same Things?

1. What recurring struggle discourages you most?

2. How does shame affect your response to failure?

3. What does persistence in faith look like?

Chapter 10 — God, Can You Still Use Me After What I've Done?

1. What regrets feel hardest to release?

2. How have mistakes shaped your self image?

3. What does redemption mean to you?

Chapter 11 — God, Is It Okay to Doubt and Still Believe?

1. What doubts feel unsafe to voice?

2. How have you been taught to view doubt?

3. How can questions deepen faith?

Chapter 12 — God, What Does Walking With You Actually Look Like?

1. How would you describe your relationship with God right now?

2. Where does faith feel performative?

3. What helps you stay present with God?

ABOUT THE AUTHOR

O. B. Levy writes from a place of lived faith, hard questions, and ongoing conversation.

With a background that bridges education, leadership, and real world experience, Levy has spent years listening to the questions young adults are actually asking about God, purpose, identity, and suffering. Not the polished questions. The honest ones. The ones people are often afraid to say out loud.

God, We Gotta Talk was born out of those conversations.

Levy does not write as someone who has everything figured out, but as someone committed to staying present with God through uncertainty, doubt, and growth. His work reflects a conviction that faith is not weakened by honest questions and that God is not threatened by human wrestling.

Levy believes faith deepens when people are given permission to slow down, tell the truth, and remain in relationship rather than rushing toward easy answers. His writing invites readers to engage God relationally, not performatively, and to discover that walking with God is often less about certainty and more about trust.

O. B. Levy continues to write, speak, and engage in conversations centered on faith, formation, and what it means to live honestly with God in a complicated world.